MW01627504

BORN TO BE WILD

By Karen & Kennan Ward

BEARS

GRIZZLY *POLAR* *BLACK*

All photos in this book adhere to "Truth in Photography" first established by Kennan Ward in 1994. All animals are wild and unmanipulated by feeding, calling, or any behavior-altering means. Landscape photos are not computer-manipulated, altered, or enhanced.

We believe in true natural-history photography.

Book Design by Kennan Ward

Library of Congress Cataloging-in-Publication Data
Ward, Kennan.
Born To Be Wild, Bears : North America / Kennan Ward.
p. cm.
ISBN 1-930700-19-9 (hardcover)
1. Bears – North America – Juvenile liturature
2. Natural History – Juvenile liturature
3. Endangered species – North America – Juvenile liturature
I. Ward, Karen.
II. Title.
QL 737.C27 W37 2003
599.78\097 – dc 21
Printed in Canada, Friesens of Altona

WILDLIGHT PRESS INC.
P.O. BOX 42
SANTA CRUZ, CA 95063
831-459-8800
WWW.GRIZZLYDEN.COM

Bear Cubs In The Wild

Being a young animal is no easy task. Baby animals require constant care and attention. Youngsters are expected to keep up with their mothers, while learning to mimic or imitate them at the same time. Romping and exploring provide opportunities to learn. Mothers teach their young about enemies to watch for, foods to eat, and hazards that lie ahead. These lessons from mom are very important, and there is so much to learn. Let's explore more about the lives of bear cubs.

Bold words are defined in the Glossary on Page 23.

Field Notes

Karen and I have spent most of our adult life in bear country. For the last 25 years we have photographed, written, and learned about bears. We have lived with bears in the most remote parts of the world like Russia, Canada, and Alaska. We do not photograph captive, caged, or controlled animals. In the wild, bears behave **naturally**, and those are the shots we seek. The stories and photographs in this book are real wilderness adventures. These wild animals have quite a story to tell.

Karen & Kennan, crossing a river in Alaska, 1999.

There are three types of bears in North America, the Polar Bear, the **Grizzly** Bear and the American Black Bear. Polar Bears live in the northern polar region called the Arctic. They do not live in the Antarctic or anywhere in the southern hemisphere, like some people think. They live most of the year on snow and ice. Grizzly Bears live in the interior of Alaska, and along the Rocky Mountains in Canada and the United States. Grizzly Bears live in meadows, mountains, forests, open **tundra** and along the coasts. American Black Bears have the widest **range** of all the North American Bears. They live in Alaska, Canada and throughout the continental United States. Black Bears live anywhere from the coast to high up in the mountains.

Kennan, a Park Ranger in Alaska, 1977.

Kennan's winter camp on Denali.

Bears are considered the largest land **carnivores**. Actually bears are **omnivores** because they eat both meat and plants. A bear's diet changes with the seasons. Polar Bears roam the sea ice in spring, fall and winter looking for seals and walruses. In summer when the sea ice melts, some polar bears move inland to rest on shore and to eat **carrion**, berries, leaves, and grasses. Other Polar Bears stay up on the retreating ice to feed on small marine mammals.

Grizzly Bears feed on roots and **sedges** in spring. In summer time they eat squirrels, grasses and berries. In fall they feast on a variety of berries: currants, blueberries, crowberries, bearberries, soapberries, salmonberries, cranberries, and raspberries! Grizzlies sometimes find sick, injured or dead animals during their travels to supplement their diets. These food sources are not dependable–rather, they are lucky finds! There is a type of Grizzly Bear called a **Brown Bear** in Alaska and Canada. They live near the ocean along rivers where salmon **migrate**. They eat so much salmon that they can grow twice as big as the interior Grizzly Bears.

In spring Black Bears feed on roots and the fresh green growth of grasses and flowers. During the summer time they eat berries and fruits. In fall they will eat acorns, beechnuts, and chestnuts. Throughout all the seasons they seek insects, grubs, and carrion. In coastal areas they also eat salmon.

BROWN BEAR "GRIZZLY" - URSUS ARCTOS

How many Brown Bears can you find in this photo?

Find the answer on page 23 !

In Alaska there is a creek we call Great Bear Creek. Brown Bears gather in the summer to feed on the thousands of salmon that come to lay eggs (spawn). In front a mother (Sow) Brown bear and her three yearling cubs walk down a trail to the stream for a lesson on salmon fishing.

Grizzly Bear Coy

COY

Cub Of the Year

When Grizzly cubs are young they have a white patch around their lower neck called a natal collar. This identifies cubs born that year, called "Coys." Coys are energetic and playful, especially if two or three are born together.

This yearling Grizzly cub tries to roll its mother to have a drink of milk. We watched as the persistent cub bothered her mom until finally the mom rolled over and allowed the hungry cub to suckle on her milk. Cubs have a lot to learn from their mothers. They stay with their moms for up to three years to learn skills for survival.

Grizzly Bear Sow and Yearling Cub

Brown Bears are 3 to 5 feet tall at the shoulder when on all fours, but can measure 8 to 10 feet tall when standing. Adults weigh 500 to 1200 pounds. Their fur is usually dark brown, but it varies from blond to near black. Brown Bears have wide, dish-shaped faces and a muscular shoulder hump. These shoulder-hump muscles work with their long, straight, designed-for-digging claws to allow Brown Bears to scoop out clams or to hollow out a den to rest in.

Today Brown Bears can be found in Europe, Asia and North America. The largest and healthiest populations of Brown Bears are in North America, especially in Alaska, the Rocky Mountains and along the Canadian coast in the Pacific Northwest. Brown Bears eat a lot, so they need large areas to roam around in to be able to find enough food. Brown Bears used to be spread out all over the world, but as people have moved in, the bears have had to move to wilder, less-populated areas to survive.

Along a river in Katmai National Park in Alaska salmon jump up waterfalls into the mouths of waiting Brown Bears. Life is good for these bears and they grow to be very large.

Adult Male Brown Bear

Survival of the Fattest !

Can you guess how much Grand Paw weighs?

Find the answer on page 23 !

Karen and I will spend the whole summer getting to know some of the bears. This one we call Grand Paw. He is the fattest bear we have ever seen. Grand Paw eats 50 to 60 fish a day.

Bears are opportunistic omnivores. That means they eat almost anything. A favorite food of the Grizzly Bear (to go along with all those berries we mentioned) is Ground Squirrel. Grizzly Bears catch and eat so many squirrels that people call the squirrels "Tundra Hamburger." Would you like to try a hamburger made out of squirrel?

Arctic Ground Squirrel

Brown Bear Mother and Two Yearling Cubs

The mom and cubs carefully approach the river to feed on the swimming salmon. She waits her turn while the male bears fill up on salmon and move away to nap. Then, she leads her cubs to the river and catches salmon for her young. Sub-adult bears (like the one on the rock) are ready to leave their mother. They'll need to use the lessons learned from their mom to survive in the wilderness called Bear Country.

Sub-Adult Brown Bear (3-4 years old)

Can you guess why this young bear is sitting on top of the rock in the middle of the river?

Find the answer on page 23 !

Red Salmon called Sockeye Salmon swim upstream towards spawning grounds to lay their eggs for another generation of young salmon to be born. Sockeye Salmon can grow up to be about 15 pounds.

POLAR BEAR - URSUS MARITIMUS

"Just Chillin"

Polar Bears patrol the edge of the sea ice where marine mammals such as ringed seals will come out of the water to rest. Seals and other small marine mammals are their primary food.

Do you know why this bear is rolling around upside-down?

Answer Polar Bears are excellent swimmers, even in cold Arctic waters. They have been known to swim for 60 straight miles. After they get out of the water they roll in the snow to dry off so that their wet fur doesn't freeze.

Female Polar Bears usually weigh 500 to 600 pounds while males weigh between 800 and 1500 pounds. With their long necks and big heads, Polar Bears can measure between 10 and 12 feet tall when standing. Polar Bears have wide paws for swimming with short, strong claws that allow them to walk on slippery ice. Their fur is colorless, but appears white because it reflects visible light, like snow and ice. Fur helps them to stay warm in the freezing Arctic and to blend in with their surroundings so they can sneak up on their prey without being seen.

After six weeks of watching and waiting near a Polar Bear den, I finally saw a mother appear with her three month old cubs. This was the cubs' first time outside the den and a playful romp was all they could think about.

Polar Bears live on ice floes around the North Pole. This area includes Alaska, Canada, Russia, Greenland and Norway. They wander more than any other bear because their food is so scarce. A Polar Bear's home range can be twice the size of the country of Iceland. One female Polar Bear was tracked by satellite for 3,000 miles from Alaska to Greenland to Canada and back to Greenland.

The diet of a Polar Bear consists mostly of seals, although they have been known to scavenge washed-up whales and eat shoreline vegetation. Polar Bears hunt by finding holes in the ice where seals come up to breathe, and wait to ambush them when they come up. Sometimes Polar Bears will go underwater and catch the seals from behind. Other times they pull the seals right out of the water. Seals have a lot of insulating blubber, which makes good food for the Polar Bears.

Black Bear - Ursus americanus

A Black Bear mom patrols a shoreline looking for any food that may have washed up. Anything will do, as the curious animals look high and low for **protein**.

Can you guess why this Black Bear cub is up a tree?

Answer

A Black Bear cub in an Old Growth Forest has climbed a tree and found itself unable to get back down. Black Bears have short, curved claws to help them climb trees. This cub learned the valuable lesson that getting down from trees can be harder than getting up. Mom had to climb up the tree and show the cub how to back down. This Black Bear cub changed its cry when it stepped from the tree to solid ground and romped away like nothing had happened.

The Black Bear can be found from northern Alaska east to Labrador and Newfoundland, south through Alaska and Canada, through most of the continental United States and into central Mexico.

Black Bears are the smallest of the North American bears, weighing an average of 250 to 350 pounds. The Black Bears' color varies from jet black with a white chest patch to cinnamon-brown, cream-white and even "glacier" blue.

Camped in the remote wilderness Karen and I saw this adult Black Bear stand and scratch his back on a willow bush. He left behind fur and scent which communicate his presence to other bears. Bears are not **territorial** like cats, canines and other predators. Instead they carry their personal **dominance** among all the bears.

How tall do you think I am ?

Answer Standing, an adult Black Bear measures between 5 and 6 feet tall.

THUNDER PAW

The southeast panhandle of Alaska near Glacier Bay National Park is home to the rarest color phase of the American Black Bear: the Glacier Bear. On a clear day when the bear is on or near the snow, the bear's fur has a blue highlight over a gray-black coat. On overcast days, the bear appears grayish in color. Black Bears in the wild are often shy, emerging from the cover of the forest only to feed. In the spring time when grasses are tender and filled with protein, bears frequent the tidal flats to feed. Here they find the sprouts of salt grass and will eat kelp washed ashore at the high tide line.

On a month-long adventure to photograph Glacier Bears, we were able to get close and not disturb the bears. The bears went about their way, ignoring us. All except a bear we named Thunder Paw. This bear had attitude! While walking, he pounced down onto the ground with every step. By doing this he intimidated every other bear in the grassy flats. His body language, emphasized by his dark black fur and big size, sent a message to all the bears and us that he was in charge!

One day while Karen and I were photographing the bears from behind a large rock, we found ourselves in the path of Thunder Paw. Depending on which of us you ask, this experience was incredible. Karen was concerned; I was overjoyed at the opportunity to photograph a bear so close to me. As Thunder Paw marched toward our rock in his earth-pounding, swaggering manner, he was unaware of our presence. He came very close to us and stopped. He began rubbing his back on the willow trees nearby as if he had routinely done this before. We could tell Thunder Paw enjoyed this very much. He moaned as he waved one arm above his head and rubbed the other on his stomach. After an extended rub, Thunder Paw went back down on all fours and walked toward us radiating his confident attitude. He passed close by, not paying any attention to us as the earth shook with every step.

Glacier or Blue color phase of the American Black Bear

Cinnamon color phase of the American Black Bear

Black Bears

Near Glacier Bay, Alaska is a rich habitat for Black Bears. In springtime Black Bears prowl this coastline looking for rich grasses called sedges. Kennan and I like to photograph and watch these Black Bears. We learn something new every time we observe them. One time we saw a young female black bear feeding in a meadow. She attracted the interest of a male Black Bear with a grayish-color fur, a Glacier Bear. The two bears played together a while-then the female decided to climb up a tree. She was able to scale the tree as quickly as a person could run up a flight of stairs. Her grace amazed me—but the real surprise was when the big chunky male Glacier Bear followed her up the tree. He was able to climb as fast as she could, even though he was so big and stout! Black Bears have curved claws designed to climb trees. On this trip we learned how well Black Bears can climb.

Some bears are lucky enough to live where salmon run the rivers to lay their eggs. Like coastal Brown Bears, these coastal Black Bears can get quite large from the "all-you-can-catch" salmon dinners.

Black Bears are mostly **herbivores**, meaning they eat a lot of plants. Their diets change with the seasons: in the spring they eat grasses and other leafy plants; in the summer and fall they eat fruits and nuts from trees and shrubs. Black Bears eat insects, fish or small animals when they can find them because animals are rich in protein. They have to eat as much as they can during the summer and fall to fatten themselves for **hibernation** in the winter.

GLOSSARY

Brown Bear: A Grizzly Bear that lives on the coast and eats salmon allowing it to grow very large.

carnivore: An animal that eats meat.

carrion: A dead animal used for food.

dominance: Control by influence, size, or superior power.

Grizzly: A Brown Bear in the interior that feeds primarily on plants.

herbivore: An animal that feeds on plants.

hibernation: To spend the winter in a dormant sleep.

migrate: To move from one place to another by seasons.

naturally: An animal behaving without influence from humans.

omnivore: An animal that eats plants and animals.

protein: Complex food nutrients essential to the diet of animals.

range: The area where an animal lives including where it finds food.

tundra: A type of land that is generally flat, has no trees and is located in the Arctic.

sedges: A thick-stemmed grass that is high in protein.

territorial: An animal that is defending or protecting its range.

Ferosha in the arms of Pascha on Wrangle Island in the high arctic Russia.

Ferosha in the den.

Answer to page 7 There are 21 Coastal Brown Bears gathered along the McNeil River in Alaska where Chum Salmon migrate in the thousands!

Answer to page 10 Grand Paw has never been weighed, but from the best estimates he is thought to be 1,000 pounds.

Answer to page 12 This sub-adult coastal Brown Bear sitting on top of this rock is frightened by the thousands of salmon in the river churning the water's surface.

FEROSHA

Very far north, on remote Wrangel Island in Russia, I found a frozen habitat where many Polar Bear mothers make their dens. Since Polar Bears are the focus of my Arctic travels and photography, this seemed like a good spot to set up camp for several weeks. With my filmmaker friend Shane Moore and our Russian guide Pascha Maryuknich, I did just that. Little did I know that we were going to become foster parents to a very special little creature.

One day Pascha and I stopped in our tracks, amazed. A tiny Polar Bear, no more than a couple of months old, sat in the snow just 50 feet away. Finding no sign of its mother or den, Pascha pointed out a word to me in his Russian-to-English pocket dictionary: "Orphaned."

We realized that the cub's mother had probably been unable to care for it, perhaps because she had had more than one cub. The cub might not have been strong enough to keep up with its mother once it was time to leave the den. We could tell the cub was cold, scared, and hungry. We were also cold, so we turned to leave. The cub followed.

Back at camp, Pascha determined that the cub was female. He named her "Ferosha," Russian for "ferocious." Curious and affectionate, she was actually anything but ferocious! As I slept that night, Ferosha jumped up on my legs, formed a pocket with the sleeping bag around her, and fell asleep.

The next morning I was awakened by the cub bawling. When I sat up, she placed her paws on my knee and looked me straight in the face and bawled again. She was hungry. Pascha opened a can of milk and fed her by dripping it from his finger. For the next several weeks, this is how Ferosha ate.

A team of Russian biologists were studying Polar Bears on the island. Toward the end of my stay on Wrangel, I took Ferosha and boarded their helicopter. As the biologists radio-collared one female bear and her two cubs nearby, I wondered about this mother. In a last hope to free Ferosha, I asked biologist Misha Stishov about leaving Ferosha with this female. "No," he gently replied, "She would kill Ferosha. Adoption is not an option for bears!"

Misha worked hard to find a good home for Ferosha. Luckily he succeeded! Ferosha journeyed to the Netherlands, where she lives today at a zoo outside Amsterdam. I have watched many bears over the years, but none touched my heart more than Ferosha.